LAST CHANCE TO SEE | ENDANGERED PEOPLE

ANITA GANERI

LAST CHANCE TO SEE | ENDANGERED PEOPLE

Published in paperback in Great Britain in 2019 by Wayland
Copyright © Hodder and Stoughton, 2017
All rights reserved

Editor: Sarah Silver
Designer: Alessandro Minoggi

ISBN: 978 1 5263 0298 4

MIX
Paper from responsible sources
FSC® C104740
www.fsc.org

Printed and bound in Dubai

Wayland, an imprint of
Hachette Children's Group
Part of Hodder and Stoughton
Carmelite House
50 Victoria Embankment
London EC4Y 0DZ

An Hachette UK Company
www.hachette.co.uk
www.hachettechildrens.co.uk

CONTENTS

ON THE EDGE

Around the world, there are some 150 million indigenous peoples, living in more than 60 countries. 'Indigenous' means people who were among the first to live in a place.

Maasai in Tanzania performing a traditional dance.

Russia's reindeer-herding Nenets migrate vast distances every year.

DIFFERENT LIVES

Between them, the thousands of groups of indigenous peoples have different cultures and customs and each speak their own distinct language. Many have very close ties to the lands they live in, and have developed highly sophisticated survival skills that allow them to live in some of the planet's harshest environments.

WHAT'S HAPPENING?

Many indigenous people's land is being taken away to make way for plantations, mining and industrial projects, and their rights are not being respected. Many groups are being forced to join mainstream society, with terrible results. Cut off from the lifestyles they have followed for centuries, many face poverty, disease, unfair treatment and violence.

Indigenous people's homes, such as those in the rainforest, are being destroyed.

CAMPAIGN GROUPS

There are many groups and organisations working to protect the rights of indigenous peoples. One of the best-known is Survival International. It was founded in 1969 to help indigenous peoples in the Amazon rainforest. Its aims are to highlight the suffering of indigenous peoples and to lobby governments and companies on their behalf.

Campaigners from Survival International protesting against diamond mining in Botswana, where the San, or Bushmen people, live.

5

AWÁ

For centuries, the Awá people have lived in the dense Amazon rainforest of northeastern Brazil. Traditional hunter-gatherers, they respect the forest and rely on it for all of their food and shelter, as well as other needs, such as medicines. But the forest is disappearing fast, and with it, the Awá's unique way of life.

FOREST PEOPLE

The Awá live by gathering honey, fruits and plants, and hunting forest animals with bows and arrows. They are experts at forest survival and take great care of the forest, taking only what they need.

UNDER THREAT

Of the remaining Awá, around 100 have never had contact with outsiders. They move around the forest, carrying everything they need with them. But the forest is being destroyed by loggers and ranchers, with about a third of Awá land already cleared. Horrifically, whole families of Awá have been killed by hostile gunmen for getting in the way of workers coming into the forest.

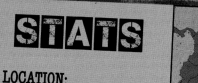

STATS

LOCATION:
AMAZON RAINFOREST, BRAZIL

NUMBERS REMAINING:
AROUND 350

THREATENED BY: ILLEGAL LOGGING, MINING, DISEASE

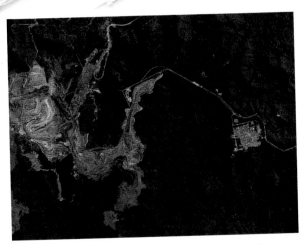

The Carajás mine in northern Brazil is the largest iron ore mine in the world.

RAIL DANGER

The biggest iron ore mine in the world lies on the edge of Awá territory. Day and night, enormous trains transport thousands of tonnes of ore from the mine to the Atlantic coast. When the railway was built in the 1980s, the Brazilian government decided to resettle some of the Awá whose land it passed through. The move was disastrous, with many Awá dying of malaria and flu. Because of their isolated lifestyle, the Awá have no natural immunity to these diseases.

Many indigenous groups from the region came together to protest against the Carajás mine.

URGENT ACTION

In April 2012, Survival International launched an urgent campaign to try to save the Awá from being wiped out. Backed by celebrities, the campaign won worldwide support and persuaded the Brazilian government to expel illegal loggers from Awá land. The Awá themselves have also been protesting. In June 2016, they blockaded the railway to stop the mining company from increasing the number and size of trains.

BAKA

Expert hunters, the Baka live in the rainforests of central Africa, setting up camps as they move from place to place. Today, their ancient way of life is threatened by the destruction of the forest, gold mining and civil war. Many of the Baka are being forced to leave the forest, often without any way of making their living.

FOREST GUARDIANS

Baka life and culture is based around the rainforest that they have lived in for generations. The Baka rely on the forest for food and for the plants they use for herbal medicines. After a successful hunt, they give thanks to the forest spirit, Jengi, who they believe is in every plant, animal and tree in the forest.

A Baka woman collecting rainforest plants that may be used to make medicines.

STATS

LOCATION: Cameroon, Republic of the Congo, Gabon, Central African Republic

NUMBERS REMAINING: up to 30,000

THREATENED BY: Logging, land seizures, discrimination

UNFAIR TREATMENT

The Baka trade fruit and medicinal plants with the Bantu people who live in villages around the forest. They are the Baka's main contact with the outside world. But the Bantu often treat the Baka badly and force them to work very hard for very little money.

DRIVEN OUT

The main threat facing the Baka is the seizure of their land for national parks. The Baka are being driven out, and forced to live in great poverty on the edges of the forest. There are even stories of Baka being attacked by anti-poaching guards who patrol the parks. Away from the forest, the Baka have no access to their traditional food or plants, and cannot pass on their skills to their children.

Singing is also a way of bringing different Baka groups together.

URGENT ACTION

One group working to highlight the Baka's plight and raise money for healthcare and education is a band called 'Baka Beyond'. The group combines traditional Baka music with British music and was set up by a group of British musicians who have worked with Baka musicians for more than 20 years. Song and dance are very important to the Baka. The women sing before a hunt because they believe it will enchant the animals and make them easier to catch.

BATAK

The island of Palawan in the Philippines is home to the Batak people. The Batak are the smallest of around 70 groups of indigenous people on the Philippines. They are thought to have arrived from mainland Asia about 50,000 years ago. But, with fewer than 300 Batak left and their forest home under serious threat, their future looks very bleak.

A group of Batak children in their village.

WAY OF LIFE

The Batak live deep in the forest, hunting wild pigs, fishing and growing rice and vegetables. They practise slash-and-burn farming, which is sustainable for small populations. This means they clear a patch of forest by burning it, and then sow new seeds. When these crops are harvested, the land is left for several years to allow the soil to recover. In the meantime, the Batak move on to clear another plot.

FARMING BAN

One of the main threats facing the Batak is a ban on their traditional way of farming. In 1994, the Philippines government decided that slash-and-burn was harmful to the conservation of the forest. As a result, the Batak could not grow as much rice as they needed and faced going hungry. They were forced into travelling long distances to find forest resources to sell, such as tree resin and wild honey.

The Batak's forest home is being destroyed by logging.

Collecting resin from a kauri tree.

OTHER THREATS

Logging companies are also putting the Batak at risk. They cut down forest trees, such as kauri trees, which the Batak rely on for the resin they sell. The government has also declared the Bataks' ancestral lands 'protected areas' with a limit on how often the Batak are allowed to hunt on these grounds.

STATS

LOCATION: Palawan, Philippines

NUMBERS REMAINING:
Fewer than 300

THREATENED BY:
Land seizure, logging, food shortages

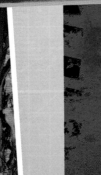

URGENT ACTION

Despite the ban on farming being partly lifted, the Batak are still suffering. They find it hard to make a living, and have very poor levels of medical care and education. Several charities are working with the Batak to provide teachers and classrooms, and to put pressure on the government to allow the Batak to farm and live as they wish.

DONGRIA KONDH

The Dongria Kondh people live among the Niyamgiri hills in Odisha, eastern India. One of India's most ancient tribes, their lives are changing at an alarming rate. The main danger comes from mining activities, which threaten to destroy their ancient homeland.

HILLSIDE FARMS

The Dongria live in small villages scattered across the hills. They collect wild foods, such as honey, pineapples and mangoes, from the thick forest that grows on the slopes, and grow crops, such as bananas and oranges, in hillside 'orchards'.

The Dongria carry their produce to sell in local markets for tools and other goods.

Dongria women traditionally wear ornate jewellery, such as nose rings and hair clips.

LOCATION:
ODISHA, INDIA

NUMBERS REMAINING:
AROUND 8,000

THREATENED BY:
MINING, POLLUTION

MINING THREAT

In the early 2000s, the Dongria faced disaster when a mining company announced its plans to start large-scale bauxite mining in the hills. With worldwide backing, the Dongria fought back. In 2013, the Indian courts gave the Dongria the right to decide if the mine should be built or not. The Dongria voted 'No' and the scheme was stopped.

An aluminum refinery already in Odisha is polluting the Dongria's precious streams.

SACRED LAND

To the Dongria, the hills are sacred. They worship their mountain god, Niyam Raja, and see themselves as protectors of the mountain streams, which provide them with water. The Dongria believe that if the gods are angry, they will bring droughts and other natural disasters. To please them, the Dongria make sacrifices of chickens, goats and buffaloes.

URGENT ACTION

The Dongria's struggle to protect their lands continues today. In 2016, the mining company tried to overturn the ban, but the Dongria won another victory and held a rally to celebrate. However, it is still uncertain how long such a small group of people can fight against a large and powerful company.

INNU

For thousands of years, the Innu people have lived in the far northeast of Canada. This is a vast, cold land of forest, lakes and rivers, which the Innu call *Nitassinan*. The Innu are experts at surviving in this harsh environment and have very close ties to the land.

Sleds are a traditional form of Innu transport.

INNU LIFE

Traditionally, the Innu live as nomads, moving from place to place. They hunt animals, such as bears and beavers, catch fish and collect berries. Twice a year, huge herds of caribou migrate through their land. Until recently, the Innu relied on these caribou for food and materials for building shelters, and making clothes and tools.

Caribou have been an essential part of the Innu way of life for centuries.

LOCATION: NORTHEASTERN CANADA

NUMBERS LEFT: AROUND 18,000

THREATENED BY:
LAND SEIZURE, DISEASES, SOCIAL PROBLEMS

FORCED TO SETTLE

Over the last 50 years, the Canadian government has put pressure on the Innu to give up their nomadic way of life. They have been settled in permanent villages where they find life very difficult. Among these communities, there are problems caused by a poor diet, as well as high rates of crime and violence.

LAND RIGHTS

Meanwhile, large parts of the Innu's land have been taken over for mining, forestry, hydroelectric power stations and road building. These activities have destroyed large areas of caribou grazing ground and disrupted their migration routes, with disastrous results. One herd is thought to have shrunk from around 900,000 caribou to just 27,500. The Innu are campaigning hard to persuade the government to give them back their lands and the right to live as they wish.

The town of Natuashish, on the coast of Labrador, is home to about 900 Innu.

URGENT ACTION

In 2012, a young Innu, Michel Andrew (left), walked 4,000 km across *Nitassinan*. He wanted to raise awareness of the growing rate of diabetes among the Innu. Diabetes can be caused by a poor diet. When the Innu lived their traditional way of life, their diet was much healthier and there was no diabetes. Michel wanted to show young Innu the importance of staying in contact with their old way of life.

JARAWA

The Jarawa are one of four tribes living on the remote Andaman Islands in the Indian Ocean. They are believed to have lived there for thousands of years. They hunt for pigs and turtles, use bows and arrows to fish in the coral reefs, and collect fruit, roots and wild honey.

A Jarawa man hunting with a bow in the Andaman's tropical rainforest.

OPEN ROAD

Until about 40 years ago, the Jarawa had almost no contact with the outside world. But, in the 1970s, a huge road, called the Great Andaman Trunk Road was built right across their land. The road has brought poachers into the forest who kill the animals that the Jarawa hunt for food. With them, they also bring deadly diseases, such as measles.

STATS

LOCATION: ANDAMAN ISLANDS, INDIA

NUMBERS LEFT: AROUND 400

THREATENED BY:
POACHING, TOURISM, DISEASE

HUMAN SAFARIS

A traffic jam of cars waiting to enter Jarawa lands along the Great Trunk Road.

Every day, thousands of tourists drive along the Andaman Trunk Road, stopping to stare and take photographs of the Jarawa. This makes the tribespeople feel exposed and disrespected. Under Indian law, these 'human safaris' are not allowed, but they continue to this day.

RESPECTING RIGHTS

Some of the islands' leaders have been calling for the Jarawa to leave the forest and become part of mainstream society. A few years ago, a plan was announced to force the Jarawa off their lands and into two permanent villages. They would have had to give up hunting, and earn their living from fishing instead. There were even details about what the Jarawa would be allowed to wear. The plan was later dropped and the Jarawa are now allowed to decide how they wish to live.

Jarawa girls wearing traditional head bands and necklaces, made from flowers, leaves and shells.

URGENT ACTION

Human rights organisations have been lobbying the Indian government to close the Andaman Trunk Road. Unfortunately, the road remains open and a promise to open an alternative sea route has not been kept. Survival International is calling for tourists to boycott the Andaman Islands until the 'human safaris' stop.

MAASAI

Living in southern Kenya and northern Tanzania, the Maasai people traditionally lived a nomadic lifestyle, walking long distances to find food and water for their cattle. Today, many have been forced to settle and take jobs in cities and towns, while their lands are being taken over.

CATTLE CULTURE

Cattle are at the centre of Maasai culture and life. They are the Maasai's main source of food – the Maasai eat the meat, drink the milk, and sometimes drink the blood. Cattle are also a sign of a person's wealth and status, and are exchanged for other foods. But the loss of the Maasai lands and grazing areas means that they now need to grow crops, such as maize.

Maasai herders with their livestock.

DRIVEN OUT

Many of the Maasai live in places, such as the Maasai Mara Reserve in Kenya, which are famous for their wildlife. Large areas of Maasai grazing land have been seized for nature reserves, game lodges or for private hunting. Maasai villages have been burned to the ground, and thousands of Maasai evicted from their homes by the government and private landowners.

CHANGE OF MIND

In 2013, the Maasai won a rare victory, after 20 years of campaigning. The government of Tanzania scrapped a plan to take land away from them and lease it to a safari company for exclusive big-game hunting trips. Instead, the area, known as Lolindo, will remain in Maasai hands as it has been for thousands of years.

The Mara Naboisho conservancy in Kenya is home to a large variety of wildlife, including giraffes, which many tourists come to see.

STATS

LOCATION: KENYA, TANZANIA

NUMBERS REMAINING:
840,000 KENYA; 800,000 TANZANIA

THREATENED BY: LAND SEIZURES, DROUGHT CAUSED BY CLIMATE CHANGE

URGENT ACTION

Wildlife safaris are big business in Kenya and Tanzania, often on Maasai land. But the Maasai don't usually get a share of the profits. One project has been to persuade the Maasai to set aside large parts of their land for wildlife. These areas are called conservancies and lie around the main reserves. The Maasai agree not to live on the land and only graze their cattle at certain times. In return, they are paid a monthly rent.

MURSI

Around 7,500 Mursi live along the Omo River valley in Ethiopia. They are one of eight different tribes in this isolated region. The landscape ranges from open grasslands to mountain forests. The Omo River runs through the valley and empties into Lake Turkana. It is vital to the Mursis' way of life.

Cattle are a vital part of the Mursi livelihood.

The Mursi are famous for their huge lip plates.

RIVER RESOURCES

Like other tribes in the valley, the Mursi rely on the river for their food. Every year, the river floods, leaving behind rich soil for growing crops and grazing their animals. Cattle are particularly important in Mursi society. If the crops fail, the Mursi can survive on meat, milk and blood from their cattle.

The Gibe III dam on the Omo River.

DAM BUILDING

In 2006, work began on Gibe III, a massive hydroelectric dam. It blocks part of the Omo River and greatly reduces the annual floods. It began generating electricity in 2015, and supporters say this energy is much-needed for Ethiopia. Critics claim that the dam will spell disaster for the Mursi and other Omo valley tribes who will no longer be able to grow their food.

LOST LAND

Large blocks of land in the Omo valley have been rented out by the Ethiopian government to foreign companies for growing crops such as oil palms and sugar cane. Many of the Mursi have been forced to leave their homes and move into resettlement camps. Here, they have had to give up their cattle and rely on government aid to survive.

STATS

LOCATION: ETHIOPIA

NUMBERS REMAINING: AROUND 7,500

THREATENED BY: DAM-BUILDING, LAND SEIZURES

URGENT ACTION

Part of the Mursis' territory lies in Omo National Park. The Park contains some of the Mursis' best farming and grazing land. In 2005, a company called African Parks Foundation (APF) took over the management of the Park and tried to force the Mursi out. Organisations, such as Survival International, campaigned hard for the Mursis' right to their land, and in 2008, APF ceased managing the Park.

NENETS

The Nenets are a nomadic people from the Yamal Peninsula, in the far north of Russia. Here, the ground is permanently frozen and temperatures can plummet to -50º C. Over centuries, the Nenets have learned the skills they need to survive in this hostile tundra environment.

Nenets in traditional dress for a national holiday.

REINDEER HERDERS

The lives of the Nenets are bound up with the reindeer that they rely on for food, materials and transport. Every year, the Nenets travel over 1,000 km, leading their herds between their summer and winter feeding grounds. They follow ancient migration routes that have been used for hundreds of years, battling gale-force winds and crossing deep-frozen rivers.

DRILLING FOR OIL

Today, the Nenets' traditional lifestyle is under serious threat. The main danger comes from the discovery of valuable oil and gas under the permafrost. Roads, drilling towers (left) and railway lines have been built across the Nenets' lands, disrupting the migration routes. If the reindeer cannot migrate, they and the Nenets, cannot survive.

The Nenets are expert reindeer handlers, and respect the reindeer as special animals.

WARMING WORLD

The tundra is also changing because of climate change. As temperatures rise, the permafrost is thawing, releasing huge amounts of carbon dioxide and methane into the atmosphere. These are the gases that are causing the Earth to get warmer. Because the ice is melting earlier in the year and freezing later, it also means that the Nenets are being forced to change their traditional migration routes.

STATS

LOCATION: RUSSIA

NUMBERS REMAINING:
AROUND 10,000

THREATENED BY: GAS AND OIL DRILLING, CLIMATE CHANGE

URGENT ACTION

To survive, the Nenets need to be free to cross their lands and to be given fair compensation for any damage. But more gas fields are being discovered, and time may be running out. An organisation called RAIPON (The Russian Association of Indigenous Peoples of the North) works on behalf of the Nenets but it often clashes with the Russian government.

PENAN

The Penan are the last hunter-gatherers in southeast Asia, and live in the forests of Sarawak in the Malaysian part of the island of Borneo. Their traditional lifestyle is vanishing fast – of the 10,000 Penan, only around 200 are still nomadic. Their long struggle to save their forest has brought them to the world's attention.

Huge areas of forest in Sarawak are being cleared for oil palm plantations.

ON THE MOVE

Many of the Penan have now moved into settled villages, but small groups of nomads still move through the forest from camp to camp. They carry everything with them in strong backpacks, made from rattan. They shelter in huts made from thick poles, tied together with strips of rattan. In the past, these were covered with giant rattan leaves; today, tarpaulins are used.

LETHAL LOGGING

It is thought that logging is destroying around two-thirds of Sarawak's forests. This spells disaster for the Penan who can no longer hunt or find sago, their main food. Where the forests have been cleared, huge oil palm plantations have been planted. The Penan have been threatened with violence by the loggers when they have tried to stop the destruction.

The Penan eat many types of fish, but fish numbers are decreasing due to river pollution caused by logging.

PENAN PROTESTS

Despite the threats, the Penan have fought long and hard to protect their home. In the 1980s, they blockaded the roads cut through the forest by the logging companies. Several Penan died and more than 100 were arrested. Since then, their protests have continued. In 2013, they won a court case against a company planning an oil palm plantation on their land.

STATS

LOCATION: BORNEO, MALAYSIA

NUMBERS REMAINING:
10-12,000 (ONLY 200 NOMADIC)

THREATENED BY: LOGGING, OIL PALM PLANTATIONS, DAMS

URGENT ACTION

In 2015, the Penan won an important victory. After two years of protests, the government agreed to halt a plan to build a new hydroelectric dam. The dam would have flooded the homes of thousands of Penan. The Penan are now demanding that the plan is stopped for good, and that the land taken from them is returned.

SAN

The San, or Bushmen people, of Botswana and Namibia were among the first people to live in southern Africa. Over thousands of years, they have found ways of surviving in their harsh desert home. Today, however, their rights to hunt for food and find water are being taken away.

The ostrich eggs are filled with water and buried for using later.

SURVIVAL SKILLS

Water is hard to find in the desert. The San know which plants provide liquid, and they also make 'sip wells'. They dig a deep hole where the sand is damp, then suck up the water through a long, hollow grass 'straw'. They use the water to fill empty ostrich eggs.

LOCATION: BOTSWANA, NAMIBIA, SOUTH AFRICA, ANGOLA, ZIMBABWE

NUMBERS REMAINING: 90,000

THREATENED BY: DIAMOND MINING, LOSS OF WATER SUPPLIES, TOURISM

DIAMOND DISASTER

In 1961, the Central Kalahari Game Reserve was set up for the San to live in and continue their hunter-gatherer lifestyle. But in the early 1980s, diamonds were discovered in the reserve and the San were forced out of their homes. They later won the right to go back, but by then, their only waterhole had been cemented over. At the same time, new waterholes had been drilled for wildlife and to supply a new tourist camp. These were not for use by the San.

RESETTLEMENT CAMP

Many of the San were moved to government-built resettlement camps, such as New Xade, about half a day's drive from their old home. They need permits to visit their reserve and are not allowed to hunt any more. For people who are used to roaming freely across the desert, life in the camps is desperately hard.

The Ghaghoo diamond mine in Botswana was opened in 2014.

The San are experts at surviving in their harsh desert home.

URGENT ACTION

Many tourist companies in Botswana use the San to help them make money. They offer tourists the chance to spend time with the San, learning survival skills. But at the same time, the San are being forced out of their lands. There are now calls from around the world for tourists to boycott Botswana until the government allows the San access to their land.

YANOMAMI

The Yanomami are an Amazon people who live in Brazil and Venezuela. They live in harmony with the rainforest and rely on it for all of their needs. Recently, mining, ranching and diseases have threatened their lands, and lives.

YANOMAMI LIFE

The Yanomami live in large, circular huts, called yanos (right), built in clearings in the forest. The yanos have space for up to 400 people. The open space in the middle is used for meetings, feasts, games and celebrations. The Yanomami hunt animals for meat, and also clear patches of forest for 'gardens' where they grow crops, such as manioc and bananas.

GOLD MINING

The biggest threat facing the Yanomami has been gold mining on their lands. In the 1980s, up to 40,000 gold miners entered the forest, destroying villages and passing on diseases, such as flu and malaria, which wiped out about one-fifth of the Yanomami. After a long protest campaign, the miners were expelled, but the problems have not gone away. Hundreds of gold miners are still working illegally on Yanomami land.

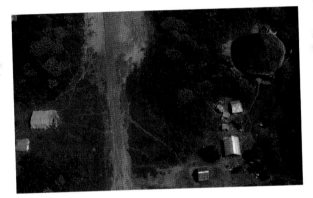

An illegal goldminers' camp next to a Yanomami village.

STATS

LOCATION:
BRAZIL, VENEZUELA

NUMBERS REMAINING:
AROUND 35,000

THREATENED BY: GOLD MINING, DISEASE, LAND SEIZURES

IN FUTURE

The Yanomami have fought hard to protect their lands. In 2004, groups from different parts of Brazil set up their own organisation, called Hutukara (which means 'part of the sky from which the Earth was born'). Its aim is to protect Yanomami land rights and to run education and healthcare projects for the Yanomami. In 2011, the Yanomami in Venezuela set up their own organisation called Horonami.

Davi Yanomami visited London, UK, in 2009.

URGENT ACTION

In 2015, Yanomami leader, Davi Yanomami, was awarded the Order of Cultural Merit, one of Brazil's top honours. Since the 1980s, Davi has led the Yanomami's struggle to protect their forest home, after many members of his own family were killed by diseases passed on by outsiders. He still travels around the world, raising awareness of the Yanomami.

GLOSSARY

ANCESTRAL
About or belonging to our ancestors from long ago.

BAUXITE
Rock that is a source of the metal aluminium.

BIG-GAME
Large animals that are hunted for sport.

BLOCKADE
A way of sealing off a place so that people or goods cannot get through.

BOYCOTT
Refuse to buy goods from a place as a form of protest.

CIVIL WAR
A war between people of the same country.

CLIMATE CHANGE
A change in the climate of the world, largely caused by the increase in the world's temperature.

COMPENSATION
Something, usually money, offered to someone to make up for a loss or injury that they have suffered.

CONSERVATION
The protection of the natural world and its wildlife.

DIABETES
An illness that can be caused by eating a poor diet.

EVICT
Force someone to leave their home or land.

GAME LODGE
A place for people to stay in when they are on safari or hunting big-game.

HUNTER-GATHERER
Someone who hunts animals for meat, and gathers wild foods, such as roots, fruits and berries.

HYDROELECTRIC
Something that uses the power of water to create electricity.

IMMUNITY
A person's natural ability to fight off disease.

INDIGENOUS
People who were among the first to live in a region.

IRON ORE
Rock that is a source of the metal iron.

LOBBY
To try to influence law-makers on an issue.

LOGGER
A person who works cutting down trees for timber.

MAINSTREAM
The culture that is seen by most people as 'normal'.

MANIOC
A root vegetable that is often eaten in similar ways to potatoes.

MIGRATE
Travel or move to another place.

NOMADS
People who move from place to place in search of food and water for their animals.

OIL PALM
A type of palm tree with fruits that produce palm oil.

PERMAFROST
Ground that is permanently frozen, often to a great depth.

PLANTATION
A huge farm on which crops, such as coffee, sugar and bananas are grown.

POACHER
A person who hunts and catches animals illegally (against the law).

RANCHER
A person who works on a ranch (a large cattle farm).

RATTAN
A climbing palm plant that has tough stems used for making baskets and furniture.

RESETTLE
To move or be moved to a different place.

SAGO
A starchy food from the sago palm plant, used in puddings and for thickening food.

TARPAULIN
A large sheet of hard-wearing, waterproof material.

TUNDRA
A vast, treeless zone in the far north of North America, Europe and Asia.

LOCATION MAP

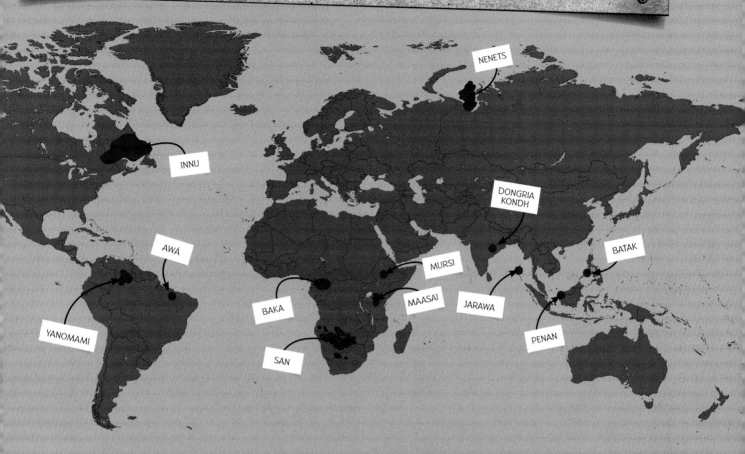

NENETS

INNU

DONGRIA KONDH

AWÁ

BATAK

MURSI

YANOMAMI

BAKA

MAASAI

JARAWA

SAN

PENAN

FURTHER INFORMATION

www.survivalinternational.org
The website of Survival International, an organisation that champions the rights of indigenous people around the world.

www.amnesty.org/en/what-we-do/indigenous-peoples/
Amnesty International campaigns for human rights, including working with indigenous people to help protect their lives and lands.

www.iwgia.org/en/
The website of the International Work Group for Indigenous Affairs which helps to support indigenous people across the globe.

INDEX